Confessions of a DEEP FRY Master

Felicia Turrentine Daniel

CONFESSIONS OF A DEEP FRY MASTER

CONFESSIONS OF A DEEP FRY MASTER

#FryYourAssOff

Felicia Turrentine Daniel

Copyright © 2016 by Felicia Turrentine Daniel.

Library of Congress Control Number:		2016905970
ISBN:	Hardcover	978-1-5144-8458-6
	Softcover	978-1-5144-8457-9
	eBook	978-1-5144-8456-2

All rights reserved. No part of this book may be reproduced or transmitted in any form or by any means, electronic or mechanical, including photocopying, recording, or by any information storage and retrieval system, without permission in writing from the copyright owner.

Any people depicted in stock imagery provided by Thinkstock are models, and such images are being used for illustrative purposes only.
Certain stock imagery © Thinkstock.

Rev. date: 05/06/2016

Xlibris
1-888-795-4274
www.Xlibris.com
735310

CONTENTS

1. THE BASICS

2. CARNIVAL CONCOCTIONS
   Chopped BBQ on a Stick 3
   Deep Fried Mac-N-Cheese Bites..4
   Deep Fried Steak Fingers 6
   Deep Fried Sweet Potato Bites...7
   Strawberry Shortcake Bites..9
   Sweet Apple Bites 11
   Aiden's Deep Fried Surprise Cotton Candy Cupcakes................13

3. OVER THE TOP SURPRISES
   Bacon Stuffed Cream Cheese Cinnamon Rolls 15
   Deep Fried Double Decker Stuffed Pizza 17
   Deep Fried Snickers Cookies Drops..18
   "Not So Sloppy" Joes..20
   "Flaming Hot" Chicken Wings/Tenders......................................22
   Chicken Fried Bacon 24

4. HOMESTYLE GOODNESS
   Crispy Quiche Bites 25
   Deep Fried Loaded Potato Salad...27
   Deep Fried Double Stuffed Ravioli...29
   Tempura Vegetables..31
   Pan Fried Brussels Sprouts 32
   Deep Fried Ribs...33
   The Best BLT in the South...34
   Thank You 39

Confessions of a Deep Fry Master

This book is the inspiration of years of watching what creative concoctions can come out of the deep fryer. After many years of working in the family business, started by my FAVORITE uncle, at the state fair in our home state of North Carolina; I have been inspired to create many different dishes while watching the smiles on the hungry faces of many friends, family and customers. After experiences on several television shows including Destination America's Deep Fried Masters, and The Steve Harvey Show, I decided to answer the question that a lot of our customers have asked over the years…. How do you do that? In the book, I have made deep frying simple for those beginners, but stepped it up for those more experienced fryers. This journey has taught me you are only limited by your creativity. So have fun and Keep Frying!!

THE BASICS

There are several basic essentials that any good cook needs to begin their deep frying journey. From the proper oil to the best coating, here are a few tips on how to achieve that golden fried goodness.

SAFTEY FIRST

Cooking with hot oil can be very dangerous!! Please be sure to cook on a level service with plenty of ventilation. Also be sure to have a non-water based fire extinguisher or some baking soda on hand.

Oils

    My experience has taught me to use multipurpose items in my kitchen. Typically, the best oil to use in a deep fryer tends to be peanut oil, however, vegetable oil works great for me. With it's clarity and high burn temperature, vegetable oil works great for those with peanut allergies and is cost effective.

Coatings

    There are many different types of coatings that can be used to make those delicious deep fried delights extra special. The trick is to find the best coating for the job. This is a great way to be creative. Try experimenting with your favorite cracker or cookie to flour tortillas and waffle batter. Almost anything can be used, just use your imagination.

Cooking Vessels

Although deep-frying is typically done in a fryer, you don't have to make a special purchase if you don't own one. A deep stockpot or Dutch oven works great. Even a deep skillet or wok is a wonderful substitute. Some other items can be pan fried in a simple skillet right out of your kitchen cabinet, no new equipment required.

Temperature Gauge

A good thermometer is a must. Unless you are an experienced deep fryer who can properly gauge the temperature of the oil, a thermometer is an essential piece of kitchen equipment to have. If the oil is too hot or cool, you can burn the entire dish or completely saturate it with oil.

Chopped BBQ on a Stick

This recipe is for my BBQ lovers who just need a quick fix. Using easy ingredients makes this a great treat for all!!

Ingredients

3-4 cups of your favorite chopped BBQ
1-8oz-package cornbread mix
1 egg
1/3-cup milk
6 heavyweight wooden sticks

1. Heat fryer oil to 325°
2. On a cookie sheet lined with waxed or parchment paper, separate BBQ into 6 oblong shapes (similar to that of a Twinkie)
3. Insert 1 wooden stick into each serving of BBQ and place tray into the refrigerator to cool.
4. In a small bowl, mix cornbread mix, milk, and egg thoroughly.
5. One at a time, dip the BBQ sticks with the cornbread mixture, being sure to completely cover all sides.
6. Place 2-3 BBQ sticks in the fryer and allow to cook at least 1 minute on each side until golden brown.
7. Remove from fryer and allow any excess oil to drain and serve.

P.S.… Try this with your favorites to dip…BBQ sauce, hot sauce, or even a drizzle of honey to make it your own!

Deep Fried Mac-N-Cheese Bites

This recipe has been our most requested and best seller at many events that we've hosted. There are several different variations that you can do to take this dish from a simple snack to an elegant appetizer or side dish.

<u>Ingredients</u>

1-8oz box macaroni noodles, cooked and drained
2 cups pre-made cheese sauce
1 cup shredded cheese blend (I like to use cheddar, Colby, muenster, and asiago)
1-2 cups Japanese breadcrumbs
1-1/2 cups pasta sauce
¼ cup hot sauce (preferably Texas Pete)
¼ tsp basil
¼ tsp oregano
Seasoned Salt

1. Heat oil in deep fryer or deep skillet to 350 degrees.
2. In a medium size bowl, combine cooled macaroni noodles, half of the cheese sauce and all of the shredded cheese. Mix thoroughly by hand.
3. Pour breadcrumbs into a separate bowl.
4. Using the noodle mixture, form a golf ball size bite in the palm of your hands, being careful not to squeeze too hard and squeeze out the cheese!!
5. One at a time, place the bites in the breadcrumbs and carefully coat them. Set them aside until they are all coated.

6. Place in refrigerator approximately 10 minutes to allow them to set up.
7. In a medium saucepan, mix pasta sauce, remaining cheese sauce, basil, oregano, and hot sauce. Mix well and allow to simmer.
8. Remove Bites from refrigerator and carefully place 4-5 at a time in the fryer, being careful not to overcrowd the fryer.
9. Watch these closely, allowing them to cook 45 seconds to 1 minute, just until golden brown. Remove from fryer and drain.
10. Sprinkle bites with seasoned salt and serve with cheese sauce on the side.
11. ENJOY!!

Deep Fried Steak Fingers

Traditionally, chicken fingers are a staple on many dinner tables. However, sometimes it's fun to change it up a bit from the norm. This recipe gives you some variety for my steak lovers.

Ingredients

1-1 ½ lbs flank steak
1 cup cornstarch
1 cup AP flour
1 tsp garlic powder
1 tsp ground black pepper
1 tsp onion powder
1 tsp seasoned salt
1 egg

1. Cut steak into 2inch long strips.
2. Mix garlic powder, black pepper, onion powder, and seasoned salt.
3. Season steaks well, add remaining seasoning to flour and blend.
4. Heat oil to 350
5. Pour cornstarch in 1 oblong container, coat steak strips.
6. Dip steak strips into beaten egg.
7. Coat steak strips in flour mixture and set aside.
8. Carefully place a few strips at a time in fryer, cooking until golden brown.
9. Remove strips from fryer and allow excess oil to drain.
10. Serve strips alone or with your favorite sauce for dipping!

Deep Fried Sweet Potato Bites

I LOVE sweet potato pie!!! This recipe is a quick variation of sweet potato pie is easy to prepare; a treat that is sure to please and will definitely cure those sweet holiday cravings.

Ingredients

2-3 medium size sweet potatoes, peeled and baked
1 cup sugar
1 tsp vanilla extract
1 tsp nutmeg
1 tsp cinnamon
½ cup condensed milk
1 egg, beaten
2-3 cups graham cracker crumbs
2 cups waffle batter mix
1 cup water

1. Mash sweet potatoes until smooth.
2. Add sugar, egg, and vanilla extract. Mix well
3. Add nutmeg, cinnamon, and condensed milk, stir until smooth.
4. Pour mixture into shallow pan, spread evenly in pan.
5. Place pan in freezer for 30 minutes, allow to set.
6. Heat oil i8n fryer to 325°
7. In a medium size bowl, combine waffle batter mix and water until smooth.
8. Using a small ice cream scoop or melon ball scoop, portion out scoops of the sweet potato mixture.

9. Roll the bites in graham cracker crumbs, being sure to evenly coat all sides.
10. Coat several of the scoops at a time in the batter mix and carefully place them in the fryer.
11. Allow them to cook 1-2 minutes, until golden brown.
12. Remove the bites from the fryer and allow any excess oil to drain.
13. Sprinkle with cinnamon sugar and serve.

Strawberry Shortcake Bites

Strawberry Shortcake has always been a favorite of many people. This variation adds a twist to the norm, with warm strawberry bites; this dessert will soon become a new favorite!

Ingredients

1 pound strawberries, cleaned and stemmed
1 frozen pound cake loaf
1-½ cups powdered sugar
1-pint heavy whipping cream
1 tsp vanilla extract

1. Heat oil to 350°
2. Pour cream into a chilled metal bowl. Whip until soft peaks form.
3. Add vanilla and powdered sugar, reserving 1 tbsp.
4. Place whipped cream in refrigerator to chill.
5. In food processor, grind pound cake until crumb texture is reached.
6. Taking a handful of cake crumbs, completely cover 1 strawberry at a time, applying pressure to ensure that the crumbs adhere.
7. Place 3-4 strawberries at a time in fryer, cooking on 1-2 minutes until golden brown.
8. Remove from the fryer and allow any excess oil to drain.
9. Sprinkle strawberries with powdered sugar and top whipped cream.

Sweet Apple Bites

These simple sweet treats are easy to fix and disappear just as fast as you can make them!

Ingredients

1-can crescent roll dough
1-12oz can apple pie filling
1 tsp cinnamon
2 tbsp granulated sugar
¼ cup powdered sugar
1cup caramel sauce

1. Heat oil to 350°
2. Pour apples into bowl; cut any large apple slices into 1-2 inch pieces.
3. Roll out crescent roll dough on parchment paper.
4. Spoon approximately 1 tsp of apple pie filling onto each crescent roll triangle.
5. Gather the edges and pinch to close.
6. Place bites in fryer and cook until golden brown.
7. Combine cinnamon and granulated sugar and set aside.
8. Remove bites from fryer and allow any excess oil to drain.
9. Sprinkle with cinnamon sugar mixture and powdered sugar.
10. Serve with caramel sauce on the side for dipping.

Aiden's Deep Fried Surprise Cotton Candy Cupcakes

So my 7-year-old stepson is my best kitchen assistant!! Anytime he hears me in the kitchen he knows it's time to get down to business. His creativeness inspires me in the kitchen and keeps me young and full of laughter. He put a lot of time and energy into adding his own twist to this recipe. Gotta love my Aiden ♥

Ingredients

2 tbsp cotton candy sugar mix
1 box vanilla cake mix
2 large eggs
1/3-cup oil
3 cups water
1 canister pre-made vanilla frosting
1 bag cotton candy
1-1/2 cups pre-made waffle mix
Powdered sugar
Whipped cream
Assorted sprinkles
Miniature muffin pan (makes 24 cupcakes at a time)

1. Preheat oven to 350°
2. Combine cake mix, eggs, oil, 1-cup water, and cotton candy mix (save 1 tsp for icing).
3. Spray pan with nonstick cooking spray and fill each well 1/3 the way.
4. Bake for 10-12 minutes, until toothpick comes out clean

5. Remove cupcakes from oven and place in refrigerator to cool quickly.
6. Mix icing and remaining cotton candy mix.
7. After icing each cupcake, place them on a baking sheet and place in the freezer for at least 30 minutes.
8. Heat oil to 350°.
9. In a medium size bowl, combine waffle mix and water, stir until smooth.
10. Remove cupcakes from freezer, dipping them in waffle mix coating completely.
11. Place 3-4 into the fryer at a time stirring constantly, cooking until golden brown.
12. Remove from fryer and top with powdered sugar, a little whipped cream, sprinkles, and a fluff of colorful cotton candy!

Bacon Stuffed Cream Cheese Cinnamon Rolls

Funny how bacon finds it's way into almost anything! With that craveable salty/sweet connection, these treats are sure to please.

Ingredients

6 strips precooked bacon
1 8oz can crescent rolls
1 tsp cinnamon
1 tbsp granulated sugar
1 stick butter, ½ of stick melted
1 8oz block cream cheese
1 tsp vanilla extract
1 ½ cups plus 1 tbsp powdered sugar
1-cup water
2-3 cups waffle batter mix

1. Preheat oven to 350°
2. Unroll crescent roll dough onto parchment paper
3. Mix cinnamon and sugar together and pour generously over dough
4. Pour melted butter over dough and gently massage into dough.
5. Place strips of bacon lengthwise on top of butter mixture.
6. Carefully using parchment paper, roll dough back together.
7. Place in refrigerator for 10 minutes to cool.
8. Remove roll from refrigerator and slice into 1-½ inch circles.
9. Place rolls on a lined baking sheet and bake for 5-7 minutes.

10. Remove rolls from the oven and place in the freezer and allow to cool.
11. Blend water and batter mix and set aside.
12. Blend cream cheese, vanilla, butter, and 1 ½ cup powdered sugar until smooth
13. Remove rolls from freezer and coat completely with batter mix.
14. Place 2-3 rolls in the fryer at a time, frying approximately 1 minute on each side.
15. Remove rolls from fryer, sprinkle with cinnamon sugar, powdered sugar and serve with cream cheese icing.

Deep Fried Double Decker Stuffed Pizza

Ok… so this recipe was inspired by that late night craving for fresh, hot pizza after a long night out and nothing was open. But, after a look in the fridge, I discovered leftover pizza . . . but what to do with it???

Ingredients

Slices of pizza (Any type, frozen, leftover, fresh. Must be an even number of slices)
Canned crescent roll dough (Or any sheet pastry dough)
1 cup shredded cheese (Mozzarella, Provolone, even Muenster work great!)
Extra marinara sauce for dipping (optional)

1. Heat fryer oil to 325°
2. Roll out dough on a flat surface.
3. Divide dough into 2 sections vertically and sprinkle with shredded cheese.
4. Place 1 slice of pizza in the center of each section of dough, toppings-side up.
5. Sprinkle shredded cheese on top of the pizza slice and top with remaining slice, topping-side down.
6. Fold dough over pizza slices and pinch to seal them closed.
7. Carefully place the slices in the fryer
8. Cook 1-2 minutes on each side until golden brown.
9. Place slices on paper towels and allow any excess oil to drain.
10. Serve with warm marinara sauce for dipping.

Deep Fried Snickers Cookies Drops

This treat blends two of my favorite treats . . .
chocolate chip cookies and candy bars.
It's AMAZING what you can do in the fryer!

Ingredients

1 roll chocolate chip cookie dough
12 miniature Snickers candy bars
1-cup water
2 ½ cups waffle batter mix
Powdered sugar
Caramel Sauce
Chocolate Sauce

1. Preheat oven to 350°
2. Cut cookie dough into 12 portions
3. Press cookie dough portions flat and place 1 piece of candy in the center of each cookie.
4. Roll cookie dough around candy piece, being sure to completely cover all of the candy.
5. Using as 12 count muffin tin, place 1 cookie dough ball into each well.
6. Place cookies into oven and bake for 7 minutes. Cookies will NOT be completely baked.
7. Remove cookies from oven and place muffin tin in freezer to cool for 30 minutes.
8. Heat oil to 350°.
9. Blend water and waffle batter mix until smooth.
10. Remove cookies from freezer and muffin tin.

11. Dip 3-4 cookies at a time into batter mix, being sure to completely cover each cookie.
12. Place 3-4 cookies at a time into fryer and cook until golden brown on each side 1-2 minutes.
13. Remove cookies from fryer and allow to drain.
14. Sprinkle with powdered sugar and serve with chocolate and caramel sauce on the side.

"Not So Sloppy" Joes

Who doesn't love Sloppy Joes… everyone does!! This recipe turns a classic family dinner into a surprise treat without the mess.

<u>Ingredients</u>

1 lb ground beef
1 small onion, chopped
½ bell pepper, chopped
1-8oz can tomato sauce
¼ cup ketchup
¼ cup barbeque sauce
1 tbsp Worcestershire sauce
1 tbsp brown sugar
1 tsp chili powder
12 flour tortillas
1 egg, beaten

1. Preheat oil to 325°
2. Brown ground beef, drain, and remove from skillet.
3. Sauté onion and bell pepper; add tomato sauce, barbeque sauce, ketchup, Worcestershire sauce, chili powder, and brown sugar.
4. Return ground beef to mixture and stir until thoroughly mixed.
5. Spoon 2-3 tbsp of sloppy Joe mix to ½ of flour tortilla.
6. Fold other half of tortilla to close.
7. Brush egg along inside edge to seal.
8. Place tortillas in fryer and cook 1-2 minutes.
9. Remove tortillas from fryer, draining any excess oil, and serve.

"Flaming Hot" Chicken Wings/Tenders

My craving for HOT food sometimes is outrageous!!!
Not just hot, but hot with FLAVOR!!

<u>Ingredients</u>

2-3 lbs chicken wings/tenders
1-cup buttermilk
1 cup Texas Pete hot sauce
2 tsp chili flakes
1 tsp soy sauce
¼ cup brown sugar
½ cup honey
3 cups spicy cheese curl snacks, completely crushed
1 cup AP Flour

1. Clean chicken wings/tenders and place in a zip top bag.
2. Pour buttermilk and ¾ cup of hot sauce over chicken.
3. Seal bag and refrigerate 3-4 hours.
4. In a separate bag, combine cheese curl snacks and flour, mixing completely.
5. Remove chicken from buttermilk mixture and place in flour mixture.
6. Seal bag and toss chicken, being sure to coat all chicken pieces well.
7. Lay out chicken pieces on wax paper covered baking sheet and allow to rest for at least 20 minutes or until ready to cook.
8. Heat oil to 325°

9. Place chicken pieces in fryer, being sure not to overcrowd the oil.
10. Fry for 7-12 minutes, depending on size of pieces.
11. While chicken in cooking, combine brown sugar, soy sauce, chili flakes, honey, and remaining hot sauce in a microwave safe bowl.
12. Once chicken is cooked and drained, mix sauce and coat chicken thoroughly.
13. Serve with ranch dressing for dipping.

Chicken Fried Bacon

This is the ultimate snack for all true bacon lovers!!! From bar food to the best BLT in the world, THIS bacon is #1!!

<u>Ingredients</u>

6-10 slices thick cut bacon
1-2 cups Japanese breadcrumbs
1 egg, lightly beaten
Ranch and Honey Mustard dressing for dipping

1. Preheat fryer oil to 350 degrees
2. In 2 separate containers pour breadcrumbs in one, and egg in the other. Be sure containers are long enough for bacon to lay flat.
3. One at a time, coat each piece of bacon with breadcrumbs.
4. Dip each piece of bacon in egg, then back into breadcrumbs to be sure each piece is evenly coated.
5. Carefully place each piece of bacon in fryer, cooking about 1 minute, or until bacon floats.
6. Remove from oil and allow to drain.
7. Serve with ranch or honey mustard dressing for dipping!

Crispy Quiche Bites

Sometimes some foods are not for everyone. Many people who like more filling foods like steak and burgers aren't onboard to try more delicate dishes like quiche. This variation makes quiche a little more approachable for everyone.

Ingredients

24 miniature tart shells
6 slices bacon, chopped
1-cup cheddar cheese, shredded
1 cup Swiss cheese, shredded
½ cup yellow onion, chopped
½ cup heavy whipping cream
¼ tsp nutmeg
6 eggs
Salt and pepper to taste
1-1/2 cups panko breadcrumbs
1-cup butter crackers, crushed
½ cup milk

1. Preheat oven to 325°
2. In a skillet, cooked bacon until crispy, remove cooked bacon from pan and allow to drain.
3. Sauté onion in bacon drippings until tender, remove onions from skillet and allow to drain.
4. Combine whipping cream and 5 eggs.
5. Add bacon, onion, nutmeg, cheese, salt and pepper. Stir until smooth.
6. Spoon mixture in miniature tart shells.

7. Bake for 12-15 minutes.
8. Remove quiche from oven and allow to cool.
9. Heat oil to 350°
10. Combine remaining egg and milk.
11. In a separate bowl, combine breadcrumbs and cracker crumbs.
12. Dip quiche into egg mixture, followed by crumb mixture.
13. Place 3-4 quiche in fryer at a time, cooking 1-2 minutes.
14. Remove quiche from fryer; allow excess oil to drain and serve.

Deep Fried Loaded Potato Salad

Most people, especially where I'm from in the south, are particular about their potato salad; and everyone has a favorite. This one is for the more adventurous that's served as a side dish, but eats like a meal!!

Ingredients

3-4 medium size potatoes, cleaned (use your favorite variety)
1 cup shredded cheddar cheese
¼ cup chopped chives
1-cup sour cream
1-cup mayonnaise
2 tbsp yellow mustard
1 tsp granulated sugar
2 tsp Worcestershire sauce
6 strips cooked bacon, chopped
Salt & Pepper to taste

1. Dice potatoes into 1-2 in cubes, dry thoroughly with paper towel
2. In small batches, place potatoes into fryer or skillet with oil set at 350°
3. Once potatoes are completely cooked, lightly sprinkle them with salt and pepper and set aside.
4. In a separate bowl, combine sour cream, mayonnaise, mustard, sugar, cheese, bacon, and Worcestershire sauce.
5. Pour mixture over warm potatoes and mix completely.
6. Cover and chill if desired, or serve immediately!

Deep Fried Double Stuffed Ravioli

This recipe has many variations that can be used. From different filings and different flavors of pasta that can be used, the PASTABILITIES are endless!!

Ingredients

1-cup ricotta cheese
½ cup shredded mozzarella cheese
1 tsp oregano
1 tsp onion, minced and sautéed
1 tsp minced garlic
½ tsp parsley
1 pkg refrigerated pasta sheets
1 egg, beaten
2 cups Italian bread crumbs
1 cup grated Parmesan cheese

1. Combine ricotta, mozzarella, oregano, onion, garlic, and parsley until smooth.
2. Lay out pasta sheets. Spoon approximately 1 tsp. cheese filling onto pasta sheet about 1-½ inches apart.
3. Brush beaten egg between filling on bottom pasta sheet. Cover with top pasta sheet.
4. Press pasta around filling to seal pouches. Cut into squares and allow to dry.
5. Heat oil to 325°.
6. Dip ravioli into remaining egg, then coat completely in Parmesan cheese.

7. Dip ravioli back into the egg followed by the breadcrumbs. Be sure to evenly coat.
8. Place 3-4 in the fryer at a time, being sure to not overcrowd the fryer.
9. Remove from fryer; allow to drain any excess oil.
10. Sprinkle grated Parmesan cheese on top. Serve with warm marinara sauce.

Tempura Vegetables

Tempura batter is a great alternative to some traditional cooking styles. Its Asian inspired lighter batter and shorter cooking time works great for vegetables and seafood.

Ingredients

1 cup rice flour
1 tbsp cornstarch
1 ½ cups seltzer water
½ tsp salt
1 egg, beaten
1 sweet potato, sliced into 1/8 inch slices
1/3lb fresh green beans
1 zucchini, sliced into strips

1. Heat oil to 375°
2. Combine flour, salt and cornstarch.
3. Add seltzer water and egg to flour mixture and set aside.
4. Dip vegetables, small batches at a time, into batter mixture, shaking off excess, and place into fryer.
5. Allow vegetables to cook about 1 minute, until light golden brown.
6. Remove vegetables from oil, allowing them to drain. Serve with your favorite dipping sauce.

Pan Fried Brussels Sprouts

As a child I absolutely wanted nothing to do with Brussels Sprouts! As most children, I would just stare at them, try to hide them or just plain throw them away. However, now as an adult I realize how wonderful they truly are. With so many different things that can be done with them, the possibilities are endless!

<u>Ingredients</u>

1-2 lbs. Brussels sprouts
4 strips bacon, diced
1 tsp lemon juice
2 garlic cloves, minced
Salt and pepper to taste

1. In medium sauté pan, cook bacon until brown.
2. Add garlic, stirring thoroughly
3. Add Brussels sprouts and lemon juice.
4. Season with salt and pepper, continue to cook until browned, NOT burnt!!
5. Stir well and serve.

Deep Fried Ribs

Ok, I know everyone has their opinion about how ribs should be cooked. Some swear by smoking them, others boil them, grill them and bake them. All of these are WONDERFUL, however, I always like to push the envelope to see people's reactions and this one definitely has its nay Sayers until that first bite. Any type of rib can be used for this fun variation of a cookout classic!

Ingredients

1-2 slabs ribs of your choice
8 oz yellow mustard
2 cups AP flour
2 cups barbeque sauce
1 tbsp onion powder
1 tsp black pepper
1 tsp seasoned salt
1 tsp garlic powder
1 tsp cumin

1. Cut ribs into individual sections.
2. Place ribs in a large bowl or zip top bag, evenly coat with mustard and refrigerate for at least 1 hour.
3. Heat fryer to 325°
4. Combine flour and seasonings in a large zip top or bowl.
5. Toss ribs in flour mixture, covering completely.
6. Place 4-5 ribs at a time in the fryer, frying 5-8 minutes until golden brown.
7. Remove from fryer, allow to drain.
8. Toss ribs in barbeque sauce, coat evenly and enjoy!

The Best BLT in the South

This sandwich combines a combinations of flavors that separate are wonderful, but together, they are out of this world!!

Ingredients

12 slices thick cut maple bacon
2 large green tomatoes
1 head butter lettuce
8 slices wide pan bread (sourdough works great), toasted
½ cup mayonnaise
2 tbsp Dijon mustard
2 tsp honey
3-4 cup panko bread crumbs
1 tsp garlic powder
1 tsp onion powder
½ tsp ground black pepper
½ cup milk
¼ cup hot sauce

1. Heat oil to 350°
2. Combine breadcrumbs, garlic powder, onion powder, and pepper.
3. Combine milk and hot sauce and set aside.
4. Slice tomatoes into 8 thick slices. Submerge tomato slices into milk mixture.
5. Remove tomato slices from milk mixture and place into breadcrumb mixture, being sure to evenly coat.
6. Allow tomatoes to rest on a lined baking sheet for 10-15 minutes.

CONFESSIONS OF A DEEP FRY MASTER

7. While tomatoes are resting, begin same process with bacon strips.
8. Place tomato slices in fryer, a few at a time, being sure not to overcrowd fryer.
9. Cook until golden brown, approximately 2-3 minutes.
10. Remove tomatoes from fryer and allow to drain.
11. Repeat process with bacon slices.
12. Combine mayonnaise, honey, and mustard. Spread on toast.
13. Top mayonnaise mixture with a butter lettuce, 3 slices of bacon, and 2 slices of tomatoes, and remaining piece of toast.

Thank You

I just want to take this time to say thank you to all the special people in my life who have supported me through this journey and believing in me. To my loving husband, thank you for allowing me to be your wife and believe that I can do anything and always making me smile. To my mother, thank you for always being there to listen and remind me what's important; and to both of my parents, thank you for your support. To my Uncle Bro, thank you for sharing your knowledge and love. And to my Aiden, thank you for being the best busy, bright, and attentive kitchen helper in the WORLD!! Lastly, thank you to all of my sisters and brothers (cousins and friends), thank you for being my sounding boards, taste testers, voices to laugh with and shoulders to cry on. I love you all. ♥

About the Author

I was born in Statesville, NC in March 1978. I was raised in Greensboro, where I attended Page and Western Guilford High Schools, along with Weaver Education Center for Culinary Arts classes. During my senior year in high school, I became more serious about my culinary career, specifically in baking and pastry. Through the opportunities available to me with the help of two of the greatest instructors I had, Mrs. Sybil Murphy an Mrs. Kathy Jo Somers(Mitchell); I was able to explore the art of cake decorating and I found my passion doing wedding cakes and other desserts. at Weaver, I was able to explore the art of cake decorating and then doing my first wedding cake. During the summer months I worked in several bakeries and attended summer programs at Johnson & Wales University in Charleston, SC. During this time, my uncle, who lived in Raleigh, had a prosperous catering company. When I had free time, many weekends were spent there with him working and learning how to improve my culinary arts skills. I also worked at Lucky 32 as a pastry chef for 3 ½ years after high school. Shortly afterward, I became a cake decorator for Harris-Teeter, where I worked for 18 years. I also received my degree in medical assisting and worked as a medical assistant in the evenings and any days I had off simultaneously while decorating cakes during the day and wedding cakes when time permitted. I am married to my wonderful husband, Jason and stepmother to my active 7 year old, Aiden.

CPSIA information can be obtained
at www.ICGtesting.com
Printed in the USA
LVHW030855171220
674413LV00028B/1013/J